PRESENTED TO:

_____

FROM:

_____

DATE:

_____

THIS BOOK IS *dedicated* TO THE *Holy Spirit,* IN WHOM WE HAVE ENABLING *power* TO FOLLOW THE *vision* GOD HAS PLACED IN OUR HEARTS.

OLD HARBOR AREA OF ALEXANDRIA, TROAS, TURKEY

In the Footsteps of Paul

E X P E R I E N C E

the J O U R N E Y *that* C H A N G E D *the* W O R L D

K E N   D U N C A N

THOMAS NELSON
Since 1798

NASHVILLE   DALLAS   MEXICO CITY   RIO DE JANEIRO   BEIJING

Published in Nashville, Tennessee, by Thomas Nelson, Inc.

All photography by Ken Duncan, ©2009 Divine Guidance Pty. Limited.

All prepress image preparation by CFL Print Studio, Australia, www.createdforlife.com

For more information about Ken Duncan and his work see www.kenduncan.com

Written and compiled by Mark Gilroy and Jessica Inman

Cover & Interior Designed by: Brand Navigation, LLC

ISBN-10: 1-4041-0482-8
ISBN-13: 978-1-4041-0482-2

www.thomasnelson.com

Printed in China

10 11 12 13 14 RRD 05 04 03 02 01

— Contents —

VIA APPIA ANTICA,
OLD ROMAN ROAD.

Paul's path on the way to Rome.

Foreword

BY JOHN MACARTHUR

I have always been fascinated with the apostle Paul. He is the ideal model of what faithful New Testament ministry should be. I often think he was more misunderstood and more unjustly criticized than any character in the New Testament other than Jesus Himself. The misunderstanding of Paul continues even to this day.

But no one was more committed to the truth of the gospel or more devoted to Christ than Paul. His ministry literally cost him everything, and he happily gave it all:

Indeed, I count everything as loss because of the surpassing worth of knowing Christ Jesus my Lord. For his sake I have suffered the loss of all things and count them as rubbish, in order that I may gain Christ and be found in him, not having a righteousness of my own that comes from the law, but that which comes through faith in Christ, the righteousness from God that depends on faith—that I may know him and the power of his resurrection, and may share his sufferings, becoming like him in his death (PHILIPPIANS 3:8–10 ESV).

Paul's suffering for Christ was a lifelong ordeal, not a here-and-there interruption in a normally placid and easy existence. When compelled to "boast" about his qualifications for ministry, here is how Paul outlined his apostolic credentials:

. . . far greater labors, far more imprisonments, with countless beatings, and often near death. Five times I received at the hands of the Jews the forty lashes less one. Three times I was beaten with rods. Once I was stoned. Three times I was shipwrecked; a night and a day I was adrift at sea; on frequent journeys, in danger from rivers, danger from robbers, danger from my own people, danger from Gentiles, danger in the city, danger in the wilderness, danger at sea, danger from false brothers; in toil and hardship, through many a sleepless night, in hunger and thirst, often without food, in cold and exposure. And, apart from other things, there is the daily pressure on me of my anxiety for all the churches (2 CORINTHIANS 11:23–28 ESV).

Who isn't moved to realize how much suffering Paul willingly endured for the gospel's sake?

Ken Duncan has traced the journeys of the apostle Paul as thoroughly as anyone I know. Fortunately for all of us, Ken is a superb photographer with an uncanny ability to capture the atmosphere of Paul's world with breathtaking clarity. Having been to many of those places myself, I appreciate the obvious effort and skill reflected in these stunning images.

This book is a real treasure. Enjoy it, and share a copy with a friend.

JOHN MACARTHUR
Pastor, Grace Community Church
Sun Valley, California

SUNRISE, GRAND HARBOR, VALLETTA.

Paul spent some time in Malta and would have come to this area.

Special Thank You

Firstly, I would like to thank my beautiful wife, Pamela, and my wonderful daughter, Jessica, for their love and support while I was on this journey. Thank you also to my good friend Charlie Asmar, the greatest guide in Israel, Palestine, and Jordan (charlieasmar@yahoo.com).

THANKS ALSO TO MY OTHER GREAT GUIDES:
Giuseppe Bianco in Italy (giuseppe.bianco@genevalink.com)
Azim Tours Travel in Turkey (azimtours@superonline.com)
Expedition and Travel in Greece (info@expeditionandtravel.gr)
Photos Hadjihambi in Cyprus (photos@kyprotours.com.cy)

Angela at Malta Tourism Authority (www.visitmalta.com) and Mohammed in Syria (m_khousi@postmaster.co.uk).

THANKS ALSO to Janet and the team at Created for Life (info@createdforlife.com) for their fabulous pre-press work. Big congratulations to Mark Gilroy and the Thomas Nelson team for believing in my work and helping to make this book a reality. Thanks also to the many others who helped along the journey. God bless you all.

Ken Duncan.

Ο ΑΠΟΣΤΟΛΟΣ ΠΑΥΛΟΣ

ICON PAINTING OF
SAINT PAUL, ST. PAUL'S
CHURCH, KALIO.

Portrait of an apostle.

Introduction

To capture the photographs for this book, I followed the footsteps of the apostle Paul, who is without doubt one of the greatest examples of what it is to be a Christian. What you have in your hands might not be an exact representation of each leg of Paul's journeys, but I tried to follow his travels in Acts as closely as I could to bring them to life on film.

In a previous book, *The Passion of the Christ,* I focused on Christ's last days. I was privileged to be invited to shoot on the set of the famous Mel Gibson movie *The Passion of the Christ.* Being on the set was like being transported back in time to the actual days of Jesus. It reminded me of the supreme price Jesus paid for my salvation.

I was so challenged by that experience I decided to explore the places Jesus actually lived and traveled. Connecting with the locations of Jesus' life really helped me get an even greater understanding of the reality of His time on earth. That expedition culminated in another book called *Where Jesus Walked,* and after that I wondered how anyone could not believe in Jesus if they honestly looked at the overwhelming body of evidence of His life.

Many years before the publication of the above-mentioned books, I gave my life to Christ. My surrender to Jesus was an act of faith after running into life's brick walls. I only wish someone could have saved me a little pain and shown me the evidence. Perhaps in those days I would not have listened anyway as my heart was hardened.

The experience of photographing those two previous books was challenging, but in both cases it was all about what Jesus had done. His walk, His death, and His resurrection can change our lives forever if we believe. Jesus died to pay the price for our sins so that we may be connected to God. The story is true and His purpose is real. The next adventure was to be quite different—it would challenge me as to what I was going to do with the example of Jesus' walk when I truly understood its reality and cost.

After following in the footsteps of Jesus, I felt drawn to follow the journeys of the apostle Paul. He had been on the road to Damascus—on his way to kill the followers of Jesus—and had to be struck off his high horse before he saw the light of Christ. I wanted to study his extraordinary life.

I admit that part of me didn't really want to follow in Paul's footsteps because I knew it would challenge me in my own walk with God, and I was right. Paul was a man just like me. He was not the Son of God; he was human—born with the seed of sin and prone to all the same temptations we face. Yet as I looked closely at Paul's life, I realized how far I still had to go as a believer. Paul was all in for Jesus—he gave up everything and devoted his life to spreading the gospel's message. Paul's adventures are an inspiration to all who are Christians and a challenge to those who are not.

Paul was a man who moved in the power of the Holy Spirit, and I believe he and the early Christians have a crucial message for us even today. We need the power of the Holy Spirit in our lives, and the sign of that power is a life that is transformed and impassioned for Jesus. I hope the photos and inspirational text in this book will convey the commitment of Paul, and that his example will encourage you as it encouraged me to live a life that glorifies Jesus.

Blessings for the road ahead,

Ken Duncan,

Paul: The Making of a Man

Rise AND *stand* ON YOUR FEET;
FOR I HAVE APPEARED TO YOU FOR THIS *purpose*,
TO MAKE YOU A *minister* AND A *witness*
BOTH OF THE THINGS WHICH YOU HAVE SEEN AND OF
THE THINGS WHICH I WILL YET *reveal* TO YOU.

— ACTS 26:16

I AM *indeed* A JEW,
born IN TARSUS
OF CILICIA. . . .

— ACTS 22:3

OLD ROMAN ROAD,
A TRIUMPHAL ARCH OF SEVERUS
IN THE BACKGROUND.

*Paul would have traveled down this road
into or out of Tarsus.*

Tarsus. Not a tiny village, but not quite a sprawling metropolis. In Paul's day, as now, Tarsus was sturdy and hard-working with an affection for learning—much like its most famous son.

This is where it all began. Here the apostle Paul was born, and from here he set out on his life's mission: preaching the gospel of Jesus Christ. Through Paul's dogged and tireless efforts, this small, ancient city became the epicenter of something that changed the world forever.

For you *remember*, brethren, our labor and toil;
for *laboring* night and day,
that we might *not* be a burden to any of you,
we *preached* to you the *gospel* of *God*.

— 1 Thessalonians 2:9

GOATS GRAZE BEFORE THE
TRIUMPHAL ARCH.

*Black goats were plentiful in Paul's childhood home
of Tarsus, and their hair was woven into fabric
to make tents and saddles.*

Paul was educated, a learned Pharisee who studied in Jerusalem under Gamaliel, one of the most respected rabbis of the day. Some in his social circles would have looked down on Paul's manual trade of tentmaking. But he insisted on being able to travel and teach without depending on anyone. His trade would allow him to earn his keep and preach the gospel without limits.

MAIN BEACH, CAESAREA, ISRAEL.

HE [PAUL] IS A *chosen vessel* OF MINE
TO BEAR *My name* BEFORE GENTILES, KINGS,
AND THE CHILDREN OF ISRAEL.

— ACTS 9:15

There is now no time to lose: the work of harvest brooks no delay. "But the laborers are few." It is hardly surprising that so few are granted to see things with the pitying eyes of Jesus, for only those who share the love of his heart have been given eyes to see. And only they can enter the harvest field.

Jesus is looking for help, for he cannot do the work alone. Who will come forward to help him and work with him? Only God knows, and he must give them to his Son.

— DIETRICH BONHOEFFER

SUNSET, CAESAREA, ISRAEL.

AND THEY STONED STEPHEN
AS HE WAS CALLING ON GOD AND
SAYING, "LORD JESUS, *receive my spirit*."
THEN HE KNELT DOWN AND
cried out WITH A LOUD VOICE,
"LORD, DO NOT CHARGE
THEM WITH THIS SIN."
AND WHEN HE HAD SAID THIS,
HE FELL ASLEEP.
NOW SAUL WAS CONSENTING
TO HIS DEATH.

— ACTS 7:59–8:1

SAINT STEPHEN'S GATE, ALSO KNOWN
AS LION'S GATE, IN JERUSALEM.

This is near where Stephen was stoned.

As a Pharisee, Paul, then known as Saul, zealously persecuted the early Christians, including Stephen, the first martyr. He "made havoc of the church," going from house to house in pursuit of these men and women he believed to be heretics, and dragging them into prison (Acts 8:3).

But the church couldn't be contained—the good news spread from person to person, past the walls of Jerusalem and beyond. As for Saul, as passionately as he hated this young Christianity, he would not be able to resist its grace for long. On his journey to Damascus to hunt down people of the Way, he would encounter the very One he was persecuting. And he would find himself on a different course altogether.

As he journeyed he came near Damascus,

and suddenly a *light shone* around him from heaven.

Then he fell to the ground, and heard a voice saying to him,

"Saul, Saul, why are you *persecuting* Me?" And he said,

"Who are You, Lord?" Then the Lord said,

"I am Jesus, whom you are persecuting."

— Acts 9:3–5

Paul discovered a personal relationship with God himself—no more secondhand rumor but firsthand faith. He immediately knew that God was not what he'd been told at all—that was all a lie. God was not against but for. God was not furious but compassionate. God was not out to get sinners so that he could make them good and sorry; he was out to get sinners so that he could make them good and joyful. This truth about God came to Paul in the person of God's son, Jesus Christ.

— Eugene H. Peterson

Damascus Gate, Jerusalem.

This is the way Paul would have left on his way to Damascus.

THEN SAUL *arose* FROM THE GROUND, AND WHEN HIS EYES
WERE *opened* HE SAW NO ONE. BUT THEY *led him* BY THE HAND
AND BROUGHT HIM INTO DAMASCUS. AND HE WAS
THREE DAYS *without sight*, AND NEITHER ATE NOR DRANK.

— ACTS 9:8–9

Paul's blindness meant that he had to depend on his traveling companions, and later on a certain disciple named Ananias. In darkness and dependency, God showed him his frailty. Through blindness he came to see everything—himself, the world, God—more clearly than ever before.

STRAIGHT STREET, BOUSRA.

Most likely Paul came through Bousra on his way to Damascus.

PAINTING AT SAINT PAUL'S GATE, TARSUS.

Icon depicting Paul being given sight, being baptized by Ananias,
and contemplating out in the wilderness.

NOW THERE WAS A CERTAIN DISCIPLE AT DAMASCUS

NAMED ANANIAS.... THE LORD SAID TO HIM,

"*Arise* AND *go* TO THE STREET CALLED STRAIGHT,

AND INQUIRE AT THE HOUSE OF JUDAS FOR ONE CALLED

SAUL OF TARSUS, FOR BEHOLD, *he is praying*."

— ACTS 9:10–11

Alone in the room with his sins on his conscience and blood on his hands, he asked to be cleansed. The legalist Saul was buried, and the liberator Paul was born. He was never the same afterwards. And neither was the world.

The message is gripping: show a man his failures without Jesus, and the result will be found in the roadside gutter. Give a man religion without reminding him of his filth, and the result will be arrogance in a three-piece suit. But get the two in the same heart—get sin to meet Savior and Savior to meet sin—and the result just might be another Pharisee turned preacher who sets the world on fire.

— MAX LUCADO

ICON OF PAUL FALLING OFF HIS HORSE ON THE ROAD TO DAMASCUS, THE ABBEY OF SAINT PAULS' VISION IN KAUKAB, SYRIA.

This is the area where Paul is thought to have been blinded.

AND ANANIAS WENT HIS WAY AND ENTERED THE HOUSE;
AND *laying his hands* ON HIM HE SAID,
"BROTHER SAUL, THE LORD JESUS,
WHO *appeared* TO YOU ON THE ROAD AS YOU CAME,
HAS SENT ME THAT YOU MAY *receive your sight*
AND BE FILLED WITH THE HOLY SPIRIT."

— ACTS 9:17

Without a doubt, Ananias is one of the forgotten heroes of the Christian Church. To Ananias came a message from God that he must go and help Paul; and he is directed to the street called "Straight." When that message came to Ananias, it must have sounded insane to him. He might well have approached Paul with suspicion, as one doing an unpleasant task; he might well have begun with recriminations; but no, his first words were: "Brother Saul."

— WILLIAM BARCLAY

STRAIGHT STREET, DAMASCUS, SYRIA.

SAINT ANANIAS CHURCH IN DAMASCUS.

This church is built on a site believed to be part of Ananias's house where Paul was taught.

IMMEDIATELY THERE FELL FROM HIS *eyes* SOMETHING LIKE SCALES,

AND HE *received* HIS *sight* AT ONCE; AND HE *arose* AND WAS *baptized*.

SO WHEN HE HAD RECEIVED FOOD, HE WAS *strengthened*.

THEN SAUL SPENT SOME DAYS WITH THE DISCIPLES AT DAMASCUS.

— ACTS 9:18–19

*K*nocked flat on the ground on the way to Damascus, [Paul] never recovered from the impact of grace: the word appears no later than the second sentence in every one of his letters.

— PHILIP YANCEY

DAMASCUS GATE, JERUSALEM.

IMMEDIATELY HE *preached* THE CHRIST IN THE SYNAGOGUES,

THAT HE IS THE *Son of God*. THEN ALL WHO *heard* WERE *amazed*,

AND SAID, "IS THIS NOT HE WHO DESTROYED THOSE WHO CALLED

ON THIS NAME IN JERUSALEM, SO THAT HE MIGHT BRING THEM

BOUND TO THE CHIEF PRIESTS?" BUT SAUL INCREASED ALL THE

MORE IN *strength*, AND CONFOUNDED THE JEWS WHO DWELT

IN DAMASCUS, PROVING THAT THIS *Jesus is the Christ*.

— ACTS 9:20–22

Years after he first preached Christ, Paul would write, "Therefore, if anyone is in Christ, he is a new creation; old things have passed away; behold, all things have become new. Now all things are of God, who has reconciled us to Himself through Jesus Christ, and has given us the ministry of reconciliation" (2 Corinthians 5:17–18). He knew whereof he spoke. He himself was living testimony to God's transforming power, and how a transformed life can show God's glory to a watching world more than words ever could.

PAINTED CARVING OF PAUL
BEING LOWERED IN THE BASKET,
SAINT ANANIAS CHURCH, DAMASCUS.

NOW AFTER MANY DAYS
WERE PAST, THE JEWS
plotted TO KILL HIM.
BUT THEIR PLOT
BECAME KNOWN TO SAUL.
AND THEY *watched* THE
GATES DAY AND NIGHT,
TO *kill* HIM.
THEN THE DISCIPLES
took HIM BY NIGHT
AND LET HIM DOWN
THROUGH THE WALL
IN A LARGE BASKET.

— ACTS 9:23–24

CANE BASKET.
*Made in the style of what is believed
Paul was lowered in.*

There were two outstanding experiences associated with Damascus, which Paul never forgot. One was unspeakably glorious: it was the revelation of Jesus Christ, which he received . . . . The other was quite ridiculous: it was being let down in a basket through a window in the city wall to escape his enemies. But both taught him humility—the latter because, in his mind's eye, he must have cut such an absurd figure; the former because it brought home to him his total unworthiness to be granted such a revelation and to be called to serve the one who was revealed to him.

— F. F. Bruce

AND WHEN SAUL HAD COME TO JERUSALEM, HE TRIED TO
join THE DISCIPLES; BUT THEY WERE ALL *afraid* OF HIM,
AND DID NOT BELIEVE THAT HE WAS A DISCIPLE.
BUT BARNABAS TOOK HIM AND BROUGHT HIM TO THE APOSTLES.
AND HE DECLARED TO THEM HOW HE HAD SEEN THE LORD ON THE ROAD,
AND THAT HE HAD *spoken to him,* AND HOW HE HAD PREACHED BOLDLY
AT DAMASCUS IN THE NAME OF JESUS.

— ACTS 9:26–27

Sometimes the most significant thing we can do for the Kingdom of God is to encourage others. Only God knows how far-reaching our investment in their lives may be. When Barnabas took time to encourage Saul, I doubt that he ever imagined that his kindness would affect believers for twenty centuries to come, but it did and it does. Never make the mistake of belittling the eternal value of the ministry that you invest in another.

— RICHARD EXLEY

HORSE AND CARRIAGE AT THE SIQ GORGE,
AN ENTRY INTO PETRA, JORDAN.

BUT WHEN IT PLEASED GOD, WHO SEPARATED ME FROM MY MOTHER'S WOMB

AND *called me* THROUGH HIS *grace,* TO REVEAL *His Son* IN ME,

THAT I MIGHT *preach* HIM AMONG THE GENTILES,

I DID NOT IMMEDIATELY CONFER WITH *flesh* AND *blood,*

NOR DID I GO UP TO JERUSALEM TO THOSE WHO WERE APOSTLES BEFORE ME;

BUT I WENT TO ARABIA, AND *returned again* TO DAMASCUS.

— GALATIANS 1:15–17

Acts doesn't tell us about Paul's trip to Arabia, how long he spent or what he did there. But we do know that a few years passed between the Damascus road and the beginning of his first missionary journey. We can surmise that during that time, as the church grew, Paul grew along with it, developing new strength and resolve as well as knowledge about the message of Jesus—the message he would soon carry across the world.

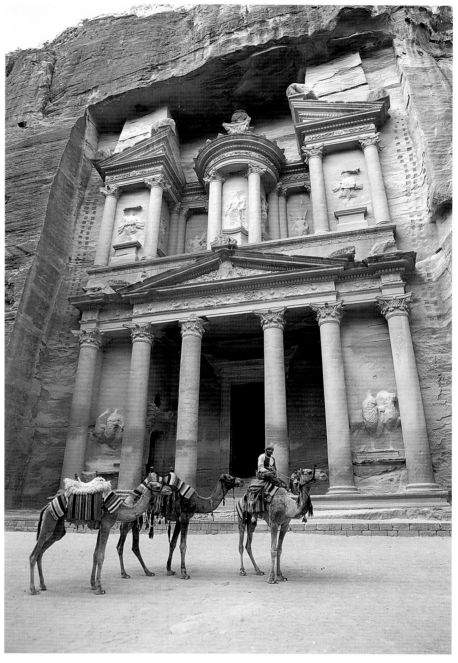

TREASURY BUILDING, PETRA, JORDAN.

Tradition says that when Paul spent time in the Arabian Desert, this is where he went.

HE WHO *worked* EFFECTIVELY IN PETER

FOR THE *apostleship* TO THE CIRCUMCISED

ALSO WORKED EFFECTIVELY *in me* TOWARD THE GENTILES.

— GALATIANS 2:8

*T*he Bible is filled with examples of how God uses a long process to develop character, especially in leaders. He took eighty years to prepare Moses, including forty in the wilderness. For 14,600 days Moses kept waiting and wondering, "Is it time yet?" But God kept saying, "Not yet." . . .

Great souls are grown through struggles and storms and seasons of suffering. Be patient with the process.

— RICK WARREN

YOUNG SHEPHERD WITH HIS SHEEP,
EL MISMIYAH, SYRIA.

Paul is believed to have spent time in this area.

AND [PAUL] *spoke boldly* IN THE NAME OF THE LORD JESUS

AND DISPUTED AGAINST THE HELLENISTS, BUT THEY ATTEMPTED TO KILL HIM.

WHEN THE BRETHREN FOUND OUT, THEY BROUGHT HIM DOWN

TO CAESAREA AND SENT HIM OUT TO TARSUS.

THEN THE CHURCHES THROUGHOUT ALL JUDEA, GALILEE, AND SAMARIA

HAD *peace* AND WERE *edified.* AND WALKING IN THE FEAR OF THE LORD

AND IN THE COMFORT OF THE HOLY SPIRIT, THEY WERE *multiplied.*

— ACTS 9:29–31

In the Footsteps of Paul

CAESAREA HARBOR.

This is the old harbor area where Paul left to go to Tarsus.

In Acts, our narrator and historian, Luke, tells us not only the amazing story of Paul, but also the amazing story of the church. Throughout both threads, what stands out most is the saving power of God, His working in the lives of ordinary people, His plan of salvation that would not—could not—be thwarted. One line in the very first chapter condenses the formation of the early church and tells us the key to the apostles' strength: "You shall receive power when the Holy Spirit has come upon you; and you shall be witnesses to Me in Jerusalem, and in Judea and Samaria, and to the end of the earth" (1:8).

THEN BARNABAS DEPARTED FOR TARSUS TO *seek* SAUL.

AND WHEN HE HAD *found* HIM, HE BROUGHT HIM TO ANTIOCH.

SO IT WAS THAT FOR A WHOLE YEAR THEY *assembled*

WITH THE CHURCH AND *taught* A GREAT MANY PEOPLE.

AND THE DISCIPLES WERE FIRST CALLED *Christians* IN ANTIOCH.

— ACTS 11:25–26

As brilliant a preacher as Paul became, the most important early communication of the gospel message came by ordinary Christians who simply shared the message of Jesus with their neighbors. In this way, Gentiles found their way into the largely Jewish Christian fold, and the churches began to multiply. At Antioch, these disciples were taught and nurtured by Paul and Barnabas, and here the believers first took the name Christians.

SEA WALL TO THE OLD PORT
AT SELEUCIA.

*This was part of the harbor entrance to the city.
Paul may well have walked this ancient stonework.*

NOW ABOUT THIS TIME *Herod* THE KING

STRETCHED OUT HIS HAND

TO *harass* SOME FROM THE *church*.

THEN HE *killed* JAMES THE BROTHER OF JOHN

WITH THE SWORD.

— ACTS 12:1–2

From its very beginnings, Christianity was no easy matter. The Lord whom Christians served had died on a cross, condemned as a criminal. Soon thereafter Stephen was stoned to death following his witness before the council of the Jews. Then James was killed at Herod Agrippa's order. Ever since then, and up to our own days, there have been those who have had to seal their witness with their blood.

— JUSTO L. GONZALEZ

THE INTERIOR OF SAINT PETER'S
CHURCH IN ANTIOCH.

*On the right is a well and on the left is an escape tunnel
the early believers would use to dodge arrest.*

SAINT PETER'S CHURCH, ANTIOCH.

This is the site of the first church. Originally it was just a cave in the mountain with many escape tunnels. The stone front was put on later when going to church wasn't so dangerous. Paul preached in this church.

HE PROCEEDED FURTHER TO *seize* PETER ALSO....

PETER WAS THEREFORE KEPT IN *prison*,

BUT *constant prayer* WAS OFFERED *to God* FOR HIM

BY THE CHURCH.

— ACTS 12:3, 5

Alongside Paul, Peter stands out in Acts as a key player in the advancing kingdom (as one of Jesus' boldest disciples, he stood out quite a bit in the gospels as well). Peter faced the same imprisonments and persecution for the gospel that Paul did, and he also experienced the same divine grace that enabled their work. (In Acts 12:5–19, an angel appears to Peter in prison and miraculously frees him from his shackles.) He wrote to Christians in Asia Minor: "If anyone ministers, let him do it as with the ability which God supplies, that in all things God may be glorified through Jesus Christ" (1 Peter 4:11). Without question, Peter and Paul were co-laborers in the wondrous works of God.

THE CHAIR AND ALTAR OF
SAINT PETER'S CHURCH IN ANTIOCH.

Peter and Paul both would have sat in this chair,
which was Saint Peter's chair.

Paul: The Mission of a Man

NONE OF THESE THINGS *move me*;

NOR DO I COUNT MY LIFE DEAR TO MYSELF,

SO THAT I MAY *finish the race* WITH *joy*,

AND THE *ministry* WHICH I *received*

FROM THE LORD JESUS,

TO *testify* TO THE *gospel* OF THE GRACE OF GOD.

— ACTS 20:24

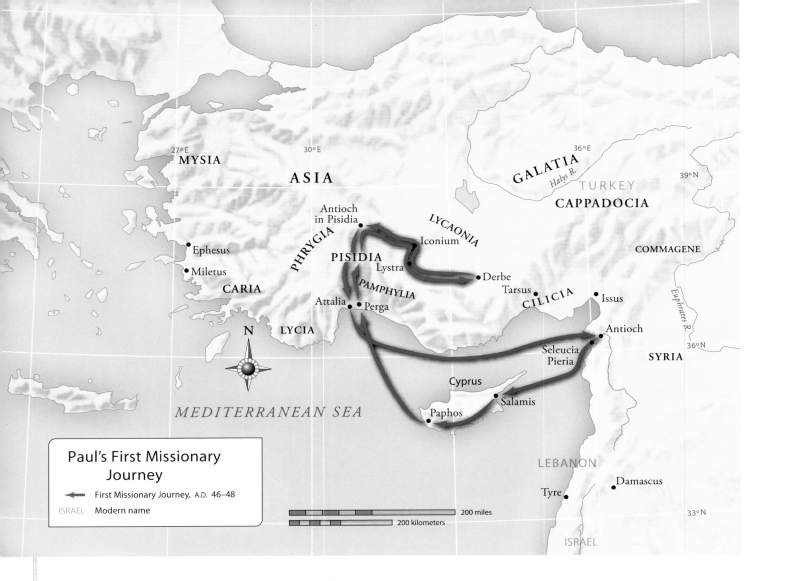

Paul's First Missionary
Journey

← First Missionary Journey, A.D. 46–48

ISRAEL Modern name

200 miles

200 kilometers

The Torch Is Passed

It was Peter who received a vision from God that the gospel of Jesus Christ was for the entire world. He declared:

I REALLY *understand* NOW THAT TO GOD EVERY PERSON IS THE SAME.

IN EVERY COUNTRY GOD *accepts* ANYONE

WHO WORSHIPS HIM AND DOES WHAT IS RIGHT.

— ACTS 10:34–35, NCV

Paul's Second and Third Missionary Journeys

Second Missionary Journey, A.D. 49–52
Third Missionary Journey, A.D. 53–57
ISRAEL Modern name

But soon after he would be imprisoned and the task of fulfilling that vision was given to Saul, who would soon receive the name of Paul. In a meeting of the Early Church the torch was passed!

THEY WERE ALL *worshiping* THE LORD AND *fasting* FOR

A CERTAIN TIME. DURING THIS TIME THE HOLY SPIRIT

SAID TO THEM, "SET APART FOR ME BARNABAS AND SAUL TO DO

A *special work* FOR WHICH I HAVE *chosen* THEM. — ACTS 13:2, NCV

NOW IN THE *church* THAT WAS AT ANTIOCH THERE WERE
CERTAIN *prophets* AND *teachers*: BARNABAS, SIMEON WHO
WAS CALLED NIGER, LUCIUS OF CYRENE, MANAEN WHO HAD
BEEN BROUGHT UP WITH HEROD THE TETRARCH, AND SAUL.
AS THEY *ministered* TO THE LORD AND *fasted*, THE HOLY SPIRIT
SAID, "NOW SEPARATE TO ME BARNABAS AND SAUL FOR THE *work*
TO WHICH I HAVE *called* THEM." THEN, HAVING *fasted* AND *prayed*,
AND *laid hands* ON THEM, THEY SENT THEM AWAY. — ACTS 13:2

And there it was. Paul had transformed from a fiery persecutor of Christians to one of their own members, and received God's unique mission for him. Surrounded by the men with whom they served the Antioch church, Paul and Barnabas heard from the Holy Spirit. With the prayers of their friends behind them, they set off.

OLIVE TREES, ANTIOCH.

SELEUCIA BEACH, TURKEY.

So, BEING *sent out* BY THE *Holy Spirit*,

THEY WENT DOWN TO SELEUCIA,

AND FROM THERE THEY SAILED TO CYPRUS.

— ACTS 13:4

Throughout the rest of his life,
Paul unswervingly persued the task he received
from God. But as we watch him start out on
this first journey, we wonder if he felt fearful or
unsure of what was to come, and we wonder if
he realized that these were the first of some ten
thousand dangerous miles he would travel before
the mission was complete. We know, however,
that he finished strong. And we know that God
was with him.

ANCIENT ROMAN ROADS, ANTIOCH.

Paul and Peter would have walked these roads.

AND WHEN THEY *arrived* IN SALAMIS,
THEY *preached* THE WORD OF GOD
IN THE SYNAGOGUES OF THE JEWS.

— ACTS 13:5

A STATUE OF ASKLEPIOS FOUND AT
THE GYMNASIUM IN SALAMIS.

*Asklepios was meant to be a god of healing. The snake around the trees seems to have
come from the days of Moses. The head of the statue would have been broken off by the
early Christians to avoid idolatry.*

Paul advised Timothy, the young man who would become his protégé, to "exercise yourself toward godliness. For bodily exercise profits a little, but godliness is profitable for all things, having promise of the life that now is and of that which is to come" (1 Timothy 4:7–8). It's timeless advice, and it echoes Jesus' call not to pursue earthly goods at the expense of our souls.

SAINT BARNABAS'S TOMB, SAINT BARNABAS
MONASTERY NEAR SALAMIS, CYPRUS.

*When the tomb was found, a handwritten letter
from one of the Gospels was also discovered.*

[BARNABAS] ENCOURAGED THEM ALL THAT WITH

purpose of heart THEY SHOULD CONTINUE WITH THE LORD.

FOR HE WAS A GOOD MAN, *full* OF THE HOLY SPIRIT AND OF FAITH.

— ACTS 11:23–24

So how can you be of service? What is your ministry to others? Where are you to spend your time? Go to the place where people are in pain, but don't go alone. Go with others who have learned how to be grateful for the good and bad of life. Go with those who can sit with others in need, even if problems and pain persist. Let your heart be broken, and rely on [Jesus'] example of self-emptying so that you can be filled by God's strength. Then you will find the Messiah in your midst.

— HENRI NOUWEN

ICON OF SAINT BARNABAS BEING STONED,
SAINT BARNABAS MONASTERY NEAR SALAMIS, CYPRUS.

Although he was a leader in the Jerusalem Christian community, Barnabas originally hailed from Cyprus. People from Cyprus and Cyrene were among the first Gentiles to receive and accept the gospel—and Barnabas was among the first to welcome and encourage them.

AND A GREAT *many* PEOPLE WERE *added* TO THE LORD.

— ACTS 11:24

CYPRUS, CLAY AMPHORAS
USED FOR CARRYING SUPPLIES.

Paul would have carried similar amphoras on his journey.

THERE IS ONE *body* AND ONE *Spirit*... ; ONE *Lord*, ONE *faith*,
ONE *baptism*; ONE *God* AND *Father* OF ALL,
WHO IS ABOVE ALL, AND THROUGH ALL, AND IN YOU ALL.

— PAUL TO THE EPHESIANS, CHAPTER 4:4-6

Paphos was the center of the worship of Aphrodite—legend has it that she rose from the sea here. Paul's visit here would be one of many times he ministered in a place dominated by the worship of other gods. As he wrote to the Corinthians, "For even if there are so-called gods, whether in heaven or on earth (as there are many gods and many lords), yet for us there is one God, the Father, of whom are all things, and we for him; and one Lord Jesus Christ, through whom are all things, and through whom we live" (1 Corinthians 8:5–6). As the message of Christ made its way around the world, it would win the hearts and worship of many.

APHRODITE'S BIRTHPLACE.

When Paul came to Cyprus, he would have sailed right by this bay near Paphos, Cyprus.

HOUSE OF THESEUS, PAPHOS.

*This house is believed to have belonged to the Roman leader who became a Christian
after seeing the power of Paul against the sorcerer Elymas.*

[THE PROCONSUL] CALLED FOR BARNABAS AND SAUL

AND *sought* TO *hear* THE WORD OF GOD.

BUT ELYMAS THE *sorcerer* (FOR SO HIS NAME IS TRANSLATED)

WITHSTOOD THEM, SEEKING TO *turn*

THE PROCONSUL *away* FROM THE FAITH.

— ACTS 13:7–8

ST. PAUL'S PILLAR.

The white pillar in the foreground is believed to be the spot where Paul was tied to be whipped. Church of Chrysopolitissa, Paphos.

The story of Paul and Elymas is a striking one. It's jarring to see the power of the Holy Spirit in Paul, how he participated in delivering God's punishment. Maybe more than anything else, though, what we see is the passion of Paul. He was furious; calling Elymas a "son of the devil."

Jesus, too, offered harsh words during His earthly ministry, even calling the Pharisees a "brood of vipers." It seems both men reserved their greatest anger for those who tried to keep others from experiencing God's kingdom.

NOW WHEN *Paul* AND HIS PARTY *set sail* FROM PAPHOS, THEY CAME TO PERGA IN PAMPHYLIA; AND *John*, DEPARTING FROM THEM, *returned* TO JERUSALEM.

— ACTS 13:13

MAIN STREET AND RUINS OF THE ANCIENT CITY OF PERGA.

Paul would have, without doubt, walked down this street.

John Mark had joined Paul and Barnabas just before they began their journey from
Antioch, but in Perga he left them to return to his home in Jerusalem. Later we'll find out that Paul
was deeply disappointed in John for abandoning the work—Paul and Barnabas will even have a sharp
argument over whether or not to let him rejoin their company in Acts 15:36–41. When we undertake
a task from God, we're offered no guarantees that we'll experience smooth, conflict-free sailing.
But as Paul's teacher Gamaliel once said about the Christian movement, "If it is of God, you cannot
overthrow it" (Acts 5:39).

BUT WHEN THEY DEPARTED FROM PERGA, THEY CAME TO ANTIOCH IN PISIDIA, AND WENT INTO THE SYNAGOGUE ON THE SABBATH DAY AND SAT DOWN. AND AFTER THE READING OF THE *Law* AND THE *Prophets,* THE RULERS OF THE SYNAGOGUE SENT TO THEM, SAYING, "MEN AND BRETHREN, IF YOU HAVE ANY WORD OF *exhortation* FOR THE PEOPLE, *say on.*" THEN PAUL STOOD UP, AND MOTIONING WITH HIS HAND, SAID, "MEN OF ISRAEL, AND YOU WHO FEAR GOD, *listen.*"

— ACTS 13:14–16

The prolific evangelist Billy Graham writes, "Sometimes I'm asked to list the most important steps in preparing for an evangelistic mission, and my reply is always the same: prayer ... prayer ... and more prayer." Traveling to unfamiliar places and speaking to crowds of strangers could knock the best of us down a few rungs on the confidence ladder. We can only guess that the secret to Paul's boldness came from his firm belief that God was with him, and from ample time spent praying before each mission.

BY TRADITION IT IS BELIEVED THAT THIS IS THE HOUSE IN PERGA WHERE PAUL PREACHED.

Here it is being used by a shepherd to house his sheep.

VIEW OF AQUEDUCT IN ASPENDOS,
NEAR PERGA, TURKEY.

This town was on the Roman road leading to Pisidian Antioch.
Paul would have most likely seen this area.

NOW WHEN THE *congregation* HAD BROKEN UP,

MANY OF THE JEWS AND DEVOUT PROSELYTES FOLLOWED PAUL

AND BARNABAS, WHO, SPEAKING TO THEM, *persuaded* THEM TO

CONTINUE IN THE *grace* OF GOD. ON THE NEXT SABBATH ALMOST

THE WHOLE CITY CAME *together* TO HEAR THE WORD OF GOD.

— ACTS 13:43–44

In the previous chapter of Acts, Luke referred to Paul as "Saul, who also is called Paul" (Acts 13:9)—Saul was his Jewish name, Paul the Greek variant—and from here on out, Acts calls him Paul.

When he went to Antioch in Pisidia, Paul began by preaching in the synagogue, but ended up preaching to the whole town, converting many, and saying, "For so the Lord has commanded us: 'I have set you as a light to the Gentiles, / That you should be for salvation to the ends of the earth'" (13:47). Perhaps it was here that Paul realized his calling as "the apostle to the Gentiles" and set his evangelistic sights even farther.

UPPER WALKWAY OF THE THEATRE AT ASPENDOS, NEAR PERGA, TURKEY.

NOW WHEN THE GENTILES HEARD THIS,

THEY WERE *glad* AND *glorified* THE WORD OF THE LORD.

AND AS MANY AS HAD BEEN

APPOINTED TO *eternal life* BELIEVED.

AND THE *word* OF THE LORD WAS BEING *spread*

THROUGHOUT ALL THE REGION.

— ACTS 13:48–49

Each one of us has some kind of vocation. We are all called by God to share in His life and in His Kingdom. Each one of us is called to a special place in the Kingdom. If we find that place we will be happy. If we do not find it, we can never be completely happy. For each one of us, there is only one thing necessary: to fulfill our own destiny, according to God's will, to be what God wants us to be.

— THOMAS MERTON

PISIDIAN ANTIOCH.

BUT THE JEWS STIRRED UP THE DEVOUT AND PROMINENT WOMEN
AND THE CHIEF MEN OF THE CITY, RAISED UP *persecution* AGAINST
PAUL AND BARNABAS, AND *expelled* THEM FROM THEIR REGION.
BUT THEY SHOOK OFF THE DUST FROM THEIR FEET AGAINST THEM,
AND CAME TO ICONIUM. AND THE DISCIPLES WERE *filled with joy*
AND WITH THE HOLY SPIRIT. — ACTS 13:50-52

The arrival of the gospel with Paul and Barnabas had a way of stirring up a lot of dust in the towns they visited—dissension and prejudice and anger among Jews and among Gentiles. Yet they kept traveling to new cities, kept preaching, kept knocking on synagogue doors. And they not only experienced success; they also experienced the kind of joy that transcends all circumstances.

ICONIUM, TURKEY.

NOW IT HAPPENED IN ICONIUM THAT THEY
WENT TOGETHER TO THE SYNAGOGUE OF THE JEWS,
AND SO SPOKE THAT A *great multitude* BOTH OF THE JEWS AND OF
THE GREEKS *believed*. BUT THE UNBELIEVING JEWS STIRRED UP
THE GENTILES AND *poisoned their minds* AGAINST THE BRETHREN....
AND WHEN A *violent attempt* WAS MADE BY BOTH THE GENTILES
AND JEWS, WITH THEIR RULERS, TO *abuse* AND *stone* THEM,
THEY BECAME AWARE OF IT AND *fled* TO LYSTRA AND DERBE,
CITIES OF LYCAONIA, AND TO THE SURROUNDING REGION.

— ACTS 14:1–6

Paul wrote to Timothy: "But you have carefully followed my doctrine, manner of life, purpose, faith, longsuffering, love, perseverance, persecutions, afflictions, which happened to me at Antioch, at Iconium, at Lystra— what persecutions I endured. And out of them all the Lord delivered me" (2 Timothy 3:10–11). When Paul talked about his thorn in the flesh, the weakness by which God taught him humility and dependence on His grace, maybe these trials were on his mind too. Maybe these difficulties taught him early on about resting on God's power in the midst of opposition.

THE TELL OF THE ANCIENT CITY OF LYSTRA.

A tell is a large mound of dirt and debris that collects over time as people build new things on top of the old. Because these cities have been inhabited for so many thousands of years, quite a few tells have formed in this part of the world.

THEN JEWS FROM ANTIOCH AND ICONIUM CAME THERE;
AND HAVING *persuaded* THE *multitudes*, THEY *stoned* PAUL
AND DRAGGED HIM OUT OF THE CITY,
SUPPOSING HIM TO BE DEAD. HOWEVER, WHEN THE *disciples gathered*
AROUND HIM, *he rose up* AND WENT INTO THE CITY.
AND THE NEXT DAY HE DEPARTED WITH BARNABAS TO DERBE.

— ACTS 14:19–20

It started as usual, with Paul preaching the gospel when they arrived in the city. He spotted a man in the crowd who could not walk, and he saw that he could be healed. When he commanded the man to stand up, and he began to leap and walk for the first time in his life, the crowd went wild. Thinking Paul and Barnabas were gods in the form of men, they could not be persuaded from offering sacrifices—which only added fuel to the fire of those who already thought Paul to be an instigator.

When Paul wrote of being "stoned and left for dead," he wasn't exaggerating. He surely never forgot this event, and it added to his theology of suffering, his belief that no physical trial could compare to the glory of being found in God and doing His will.

OLD MUD BRICK COTTAGE WITH THE
TELL OF DERBE IN THE BACKGROUND.

AND WHEN THEY HAD *preached* THE GOSPEL TO THAT CITY

AND MADE *many* DISCIPLES, THEY RETURNED TO LYSTRA, ICONIUM,

AND ANTIOCH, *strengthening* THE SOULS OF THE DISCIPLES,

EXHORTING THEM TO CONTINUE IN THE FAITH,

AND SAYING, "WE MUST THROUGH MANY *tribulations* ENTER THE

KINGDOM OF GOD."... AND AFTER THEY HAD

PASSED THROUGH PISIDIA, THEY CAME TO PAMPHYLIA.

— ACTS 14:21–22, 24

The early Christians were able to experience joy in their hearts in the midst of trials, troubles, and depression. They counted suffering for Christ not as a burden or misfortune but as a great honor, as evidence that Christ counted them worthy to witness for Him through suffering. They never forgot what Christ Himself had gone through for their salvation, and to suffer for His name's sake was regarded as a gift rather than a cross.

— BILLY GRAHAM

ANCIENT HARBOR OF ATTALIA.

It is from here that Paul would have left Turkey by boat, returning to Seleucia.

FROM THERE THEY SAILED TO ANTIOCH,

WHERE THEY HAD BEEN COMMENDED TO THE GRACE OF GOD

FOR THE WORK WHICH THEY HAD COMPLETED.

NOW WHEN THEY HAD COME AND GATHERED THE CHURCH *together,*

THEY *reported* ALL THAT GOD HAD *done* WITH THEM,

AND THAT HE HAD *opened* THE *door* OF FAITH TO THE GENTILES.

SO THEY STAYED THERE A LONG TIME WITH THE DISCIPLES.

— ACTS 14:26–28

It was done. They had come full circle and returned to Antioch, their starting point. Paul's first journey was complete, and after battling difficulties expected and unexpected, and dodging ill winds on the sea, the missionaries returned to their home church. They resolved a few disputes over how to incorporate the Gentiles into this new faith, and they taught and, perhaps, gathered strength from the Antiochian disciples. But before long, they would be heading out again to visit the cities where they had preached. New adventures were to come.

KIZKALESI, CORYCUS CASTLE WITH
MAIDENS CASTLE IN THE BACKGROUND.

This arch was an ancient sea door to the castle. Paul would have sailed past this area, which was known for piracy. In the days of Paul, sea voyages had to contend with piracy as well as weather issues.

PAUL CHOSE SILAS AND DEPARTED,

BEING COMMENDED BY THE BRETHREN

TO THE GRACE OF GOD.

AND HE WENT THROUGH SYRIA AND CILICIA,

strengthening THE CHURCHES.

— ACTS 15:40–41

"*Let's go back,*" *Paul said to Barnabas.* He wanted to see how the churches were doing. Within this text there's a sense that he felt eager to get back on the road, excited about the work God was doing among the Gentiles, and ready to continue the mission God had given him. From here, he goes with Silas, a leader at the Jerusalem church, instead of Barnabas—Barnabas wanted to give John Mark another chance, while Paul no longer trusted him, so the two went their separate ways. With a new partner, Paul embarked, eager to persevere in the work of the Lord.

THE IRON GATE ON THE PARMENIOS
RIVER, ANTIOCH, TURKEY.

This was one of the early gates that Paul would have
traveled through on the Parmenios River.

MUD BRICK FARMHOUSE WITH
TELL OF DERBE IN THE BACKGROUND
(YET TO BE EXCAVATED).

This way of making houses has not changed since the time of Paul.
On the doorstep, the farmers have used a marble slab
they probably found while tilling their fields.

THERE HE CAME TO DERBE AND LYSTRA. AND BEHOLD, A CERTAIN

DISCIPLE WAS THERE, NAMED *Timothy*.... HE WAS *well spoken of* BY

THE BRETHREN WHO WERE AT LYSTRA AND ICONIUM.

PAUL WANTED TO HAVE HIM GO ON WITH HIM. — ACTS 16:1-3

On this second journey, Paul met Timothy for the first time. As they traveled together, Timothy became Paul's beloved pupil, and Paul probably spoke of no one more highly than he did Timothy. He wrote of him to the Philippians, "I have no one like-minded," and "you know his proven character, that as a son with his father he served with me in the gospel" (Philippians 2:20, 22). Their journey together would end with Paul passing his torch on to Timothy. As they set out from Lystra, they were beginning a relationship that would shape both of their lives and ultimately serve to advance the gospel.

CLEOPATRA'S GATE, TARSUS.

This gate would have been there in the time of Paul and he would have entered through it.

OLD ROMAN ROAD LEADING TO LYSTRA
FROM KILYSTRA.

NOW WHEN THEY HAD GONE THROUGH PHRYGIA

AND THE REGION OF GALATIA,

THEY WERE *forbidden* BY THE HOLY SPIRIT

TO PREACH THE WORD IN ASIA.

— ACTS 16:6

Paul and his fellow servants were yielded to the leadership of the Holy Spirit. Therefore, they were pliable when God prompted them not to enter the province of Asia by removing their sense of peace and approval. Thankfully, they were willing to allow God to change their plans . . . . [Paul] learned to follow the leadership of the Holy Spirit one day at a time, one city at a time—on-the-job training. Let's learn from his example and be willing to change our course when we sense God has different plans.

— BETH MOORE

WILD POPPIES NEAR TROAS
OVERLOOKING THE AEGEAN SEA.

SO PASSING BY MYSIA, THEY CAME DOWN TO TROAS.

AND A *vision* APPEARED TO PAUL IN THE NIGHT.

A MAN OF MACEDONIA STOOD AND PLEADED WITH HIM, SAYING,

"COME OVER TO MACEDONIA TO *help us.*"

NOW AFTER HE HAD SEEN THE VISION, IMMEDIATELY WE SOUGHT

TO GO TO MACEDONIA, CONCLUDING THAT THE LORD HAD

CALLED US TO PREACH THE GOSPEL TO THEM. — ACTS 16:8–10

The Holy Spirit had prevented Paul's company from going into Asia, and here Paul received a vision leading them to Macedonia. Acts will pick up this theme increasingly: God Himself directed Paul's ministry. He called him on the road to Damascus, He separated him for missionary work in Antioch, and He would continue to guide him as he ministered. Later, when it became evident that Paul was traveling irresistibly to Rome, where he faced certain opposition and probable death, he would stay the course without flinching. He knew that the Holy Spirit directed his every move.

ICON OF LYDIA, SAINT PAUL'S CATHEDRAL, KAVALA.

Found in what was once the ancient city of Neapolis.

MOSAIC DEPICTING
THE JOURNEY OF PAUL—
STEPPING ONTO THE SHORES OF NEAPOLIS.

*This mosaic is part of Saint Nicholas Church, built on the site where it is
believed Paul stepped from the boat onto the land at Neapolis.*

THEREFORE, SAILING FROM TROAS,

WE RAN A STRAIGHT *course* TO SAMOTHRACE,

AND THE NEXT DAY CAME TO *Neapolis.*

— ACTS 16:11

The previous verse marks the start of the so-called "we passages" of Acts—here Luke picks up the first-person plural during the narration of the sea voyages. For some portion of Paul's journeys, he seems to have traveled in a company of four: himself, Timothy, Silas, and Luke. We don't know how Luke met Paul or became a part of these missionary journeys. Maybe they met in Troas, or maybe Luke was a native of Philippi. In any case, Luke's presence gives modern readers a priceless insider account of Paul's adventures.

ANCIENT DWELLING IN KILYSTRA, NEAR LYSTRA.

Lystra was a Christian influenced place that Paul likely would have visited.

SAINT LYDIA'S BAPTISM SITE,
PHILIPPI, GREECE.

AND FROM THERE TO PHILIPPI, WHICH IS THE FOREMOST CITY OF THAT
PART OF MACEDONIA, A COLONY.... AND ON THE SABBATH DAY WE WENT
OUT OF THE CITY TO THE RIVERSIDE, WHERE PRAYER WAS CUSTOMARILY MADE;
AND WE SAT DOWN AND SPOKE TO THE WOMEN WHO MET THERE. NOW A
CERTAIN WOMAN NAMED *Lydia* HEARD US. SHE WAS A SELLER OF PURPLE FROM
THE CITY OF THYATIRA, WHO WORSHIPED GOD. THE LORD *opened her heart*
TO HEED THE THINGS SPOKEN BY PAUL. — ACTS 16:12–14

To win a soul it is necessary not only to instruct our hearer and make him know the truth, but to impress him so that he may feel it…. A sinner has a heart as well as a head, and we must appeal to both. . . . The Truth must soak into the soul and dye it with its own color. The Word must be like a strong wind sweeping through the whole heart and swaying the whole man, even as a field of ripening corn waves in the summer breeze.

— C. H. SPURGEON

ROMAN AGORA WHERE
PAUL AND SILAS WERE FLOGGED.

THEN THE *multitude* ROSE UP TOGETHER *against* THEM; AND THE MAGISTRATES
TORE OFF THEIR CLOTHES AND COMMANDED THEM TO BE BEATEN WITH RODS.
AND WHEN THEY HAD LAID MANY STRIPES ON THEM, THEY THREW THEM
INTO *prison,* COMMANDING THE JAILER TO KEEP THEM SECURELY.
HAVING RECEIVED SUCH A *charge,* HE PUT THEM INTO THE INNER PRISON
AND FASTENED THEIR FEET IN THE STOCKS. — ACTS 16:22–24

In the Footsteps of Paul

The story of Paul and Silas's imprisonment found in Acts 16:16–39 is another in the litany of Paul's sufferings as an apostle, but it also makes for an intriguing read about forgiveness and redemption. One of the many notable elements in the story is that when the earthquake broke the prisoners' chains, they didn't seize the opportunity to escape. By staying put, they saved the jailer's life. In return, he took them home and washed their wounds, and everyone in his family was baptized.

We know that Paul was mission-driven, so focused on the goal of bringing Christ to the nations that nothing could deter him. But here we see that he wasn't so focused on getting to the next city that he would miss an opportunity to reach out with compassion to an individual. He had a specific mission from God, but that mission didn't overtake his greater calling to act justly and love mercy.

PRISON OF PAUL AND SILAS,
ARCHAEOLOGICAL SITE
IN PHILIPPI, GREECE.

SO THEY WENT OUT OF PRISON AND ENTERED THE HOUSE OF LYDIA;

AND WHEN THEY HAD SEEN THE *brethren,*

THEY *encouraged* THEM AND DEPARTED.

NOW WHEN THEY HAD PASSED THROUGH AMPHIPOLIS

AND APOLLONIA, THEY CAME TO THESSALONICA,

WHERE THERE WAS A SYNAGOGUE OF JEWS.

— ACTS 16:40–17:1

Amphipolis and Apollonia both rested on the Via Egnatia, a great Roman highway traveled by Paul. Amphipolis was a commercially significant city, a short distance from the Aegean Sea and Mount Pangaeus with its supplies of ore and timber. We don't know why Paul didn't stop there, and no one seems to know for certain if Paul had a detailed itinerary in mind when he started out on these journeys. We do know one thing: Paul was led by the Holy Spirit at every turn.

FISHERMEN NEAR AMPHIPOLIS.

EASTERN BYZANTINE WALLS, THESSALONICA.

AND SOME OF THEM WERE *persuaded;* AND A GREAT MULTITUDE
OF THE DEVOUT GREEKS, AND NOT A FEW OF THE LEADING WOMEN,
joined PAUL AND SILAS. BUT THE JEWS WHO WERE NOT PERSUADED,
BECOMING *envious,* TOOK SOME OF THE *evil men* FROM THE MARKETPLACE,
AND GATHERING A MOB, SET ALL THE CITY IN AN UPROAR
AND *attacked* THE HOUSE OF JASON,
AND SOUGHT TO BRING THEM OUT TO THE PEOPLE. — ACTS 17:4–5

Can the gospel spread, and thousands be converted, and churches grow, and love abound where Christianity is continually spoken against? Yes. It not only can; it has. I say this not to discourage winsomeness, but to encourage hope. Do not assume that seasons of hostility or controversy will be lean seasons with little power or growth. They may be seasons of explosive growth and great spiritual blessing.

— JOHN PIPER

MONASTERY OF VLATADON, GREECE.
Tradition says this is where Paul preached to the Jews.

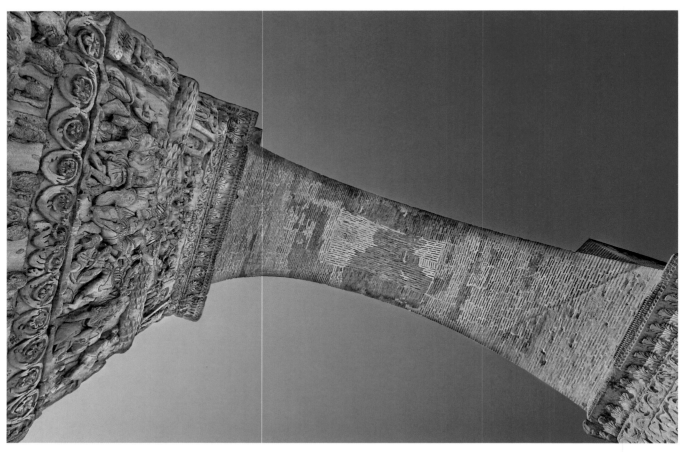

KAMARA (GALERIUS ARCH), THESSALONICA.

This arch was there at the time of Paul and he would have walked through it.

BUT WHEN THEY DID NOT FIND THEM, THEY *dragged* JASON AND

SOME BRETHREN TO THE *rulers* OF THE CITY, CRYING OUT,

"THESE WHO HAVE TURNED THE WORLD *upside down* HAVE COME HERE TOO.

JASON HAS HARBORED THEM, AND THESE ARE ALL ACTING CONTRARY

TO THE *decrees* OF CAESAR, SAYING THERE IS ANOTHER *king*—JESUS."

— ACTS 17:6–7

When Paul and Silas were arrested in Philippi, the trouble started when they cast a demon from a fortune-teller. No longer able to tell fortunes, she was no longer profitable to her masters, and so they dragged Paul and Silas before the authorities, saying, "These men . . . teach customs which are not lawful for us, being Romans, to receive or observe" (Acts 16:20–21). And in Thessalonica, it seemed that the crowd had heard about Paul and Silas—they called them "these who have turned the world upside down" and complained to the authorities that they preached Jesus as a new king.

They weren't entirely wrong. Paul and Silas did preach a new kingdom, and Jesus was a new king, no less powerful or present than an earthly one. His kingdom was not of the world. But it indeed had a way of turning the world upside down.

DETAIL OF KAMARA (GALERIUS ARCH).

THEN THE BRETHREN *immediately* SENT PAUL AND SILAS AWAY BY NIGHT TO BEREA. WHEN THEY ARRIVED, THEY WENT INTO THE SYNAGOGUE OF THE JEWS. THESE WERE MORE *fair-minded* THAN THOSE IN THESSALONICA, IN THAT THEY RECEIVED THE WORD WITH *all readiness,* AND SEARCHED THE SCRIPTURES *daily* TO FIND OUT WHETHER THESE THINGS WERE SO.

— ACTS 17:10–11

When Paul spoke in a new city, trouble usually followed. But in every city, Paul also won converts. After hearing Paul preach at the synagogue, the Bereans busily searched the Scriptures, and "many of them believed, and also not a few of the Greeks, prominent women as well as men" (Acts 17:12). Not every conversion story would be as spectacular as the Philippian jailer's; but through Paul's efforts, many did come to believe, and slowly whole communities of believers began to form. In fact, Paul would write 1 and 2 Thessalonians to Christian churches in this very region.

THE APOSTLE PAUL'S ALTAR.

This is the place where it is said Paul spoke from the steps to the people of Berea.

PARTHENON FROM
PHILOPAPPOU HILL, ATHENS.

SO THOSE WHO CONDUCTED PAUL BROUGHT HIM TO ATHENS; AND *receiving*
A *command* FOR SILAS AND TIMOTHY TO COME TO HIM WITH ALL SPEED,
THEY *departed.* NOW WHILE PAUL WAITED FOR THEM AT ATHENS,
HIS SPIRIT WAS *provoked* WITHIN HIM WHEN HE SAW THAT THE CITY WAS
GIVEN OVER TO IDOLS. THEREFORE HE *reasoned* IN THE SYNAGOGUE WITH
THE JEWS AND WITH THE GENTILE WORSHIPERS, AND IN THE MARKETPLACE
DAILY WITH THOSE WHO HAPPENED TO BE THERE. — ACTS 17:14–17

When the first disciples were sent off by Jesus into the wider world to announce that he was Israel's Messiah and hence the world's true Lord, they knew that their message would make little or no sense to most of their hearers . . . . And yet the early Christians discovered that telling this story carried a power which they regularly associated with the Spirit, but which they often referred to simply as "the word." . . . In other words, when you announce the good news that the risen Jesus is Lord, that very word is the word of God, a carrier or agent of God's Spirit.

— N. T. WRIGHT

PARTHENON ON THE ACROPOLIS, ATHENS.

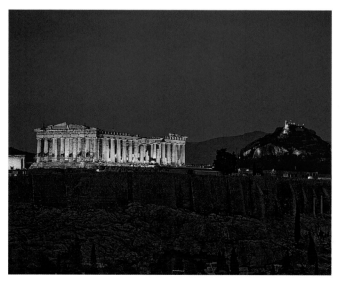

TEMPLE OF OLYMPIAN ZEUS
WITH THE ACROPOLIS IN THE BACKGROUND.

THEN CERTAIN EPICUREAN AND STOIC *philosophers*
ENCOUNTERED HIM.... AND THEY TOOK HIM AND BROUGHT HIM
TO THE AREOPAGUS, SAYING, "MAY WE KNOW
WHAT THIS *new doctrine* IS OF WHICH YOU SPEAK?"

— ACTS 17:18–19

The philosophers in Athens loved new ideas. And so they welcomed Paul to speak and explain what he had been teaching around town. Here Paul's education shows—in Acts 17:22–31 he delivers a reasoned and thoughtful treatise, albeit brief, about God as the creator of all we know and the redeemer of creation. Some of the philosophers mocked. Others deferred with, "We will hear you again on this matter" (v. 32). But others believed and became disciples.

AFTER THESE THINGS PAUL *departed* FROM ATHENS
AND WENT TO CORINTH.

— ACTS 18:1

*T*he *Temple of Apollo, built in the fourth century BC,* stands as a reminder of the ancient city's devotion to the Hellenistic pantheon, a cornucopia of Greek gods. These temples played a vital role in the daily life of Corinth's citizens—here is where they not only worshiped, but also socialized and did business. Paul would write two letters to the Corinthians, and judging by the letters' cajoling and confrontational tone, Corinth may have been the congregation he had the most trouble with. There were issues of speaking in tongues and of meat sacrificed to idols, snags that probably had much to do with the cultural milieu of Corinth.

We've seen, however, that the early Christian church flourished in the face of difficulty. While he was in Corinth to evangelize, God spoke to Paul in a vision: "Do not be afraid, but speak, and do not keep silent; for I am with you, and no one will attack you to hurt you; for I have many people in this city" (Acts 18:9–10). Even when the going was tough, Paul and the other early church leaders would meet with success, and they would keep going.

TEMPLE OF APOLLO,
ANCIENT CORINTH.

Paul preached in this city.

A N D H E *found* A C E R T A I N J E W N A M E D A Q U I L A , B O R N I N P O N T U S ,

W H O H A D R E C E N T L Y C O M E F R O M I T A L Y W I T H H I S W I F E P R I S C I L L A

(B E C A U S E C L A U D I U S H A D *commanded* A L L T H E J E W S

T O *depart* F R O M R O M E) ; A N D H E C A M E T O T H E M .

— A C T S 1 8 : 2

The meeting between Paul and Priscilla and Aquila had to have been a great day in Paul's life. He was able to work and stay with them and enjoy their companionship. They became invaluable to him in strengthening the churches. He went on to write in Romans 16:3–4, "Greet Priscilla and Aquila, my fellow workers in Christ Jesus, who risked their own necks for my life, to whom not only I give thanks, but also all the churches of the Gentiles."

Not too long after their meeting, Timothy and Silas joined Paul from Macedonia, and at that point, Luke tells us, "Paul was compelled by the Spirit, and testified to the Jews that Jesus is the Christ" (Acts 18:5). Like all of us, Paul needed good friends to encourage him and enable his work. And also like all of us, Paul could depend on God to send just the right people at just the right time.

HE HAD HIS *hair cut* OFF AT CENCHREA,

FOR HE HAD TAKEN A *vow.*

— ACTS 18:18

Here at Cenchrea, Paul cut off his hair in fulfillment of a vow, but Luke doesn't tell us what his vow was. Jews of the time often took a Nazirite vow, abstaining from alcohol and from cutting their hair, to express thankfulness or ask God for help. At the end of the period of abstinence, they would cut their hair and offer a sacrifice at the temple in Jerusalem. Maybe Paul wanted to thank God for protecting him, or to ask Him to continue to do so. And perhaps the fulfillment of the vow at Cenchrea partly explains his apparent eagerness to get to Jerusalem, so that he could offer sacrifices (Acts 18:21). We don't know the back story, but Paul's vow does tell us that he maintained a rich inner faith even as he busied himself with helping others find the kingdom.

OLD HARBOR AT CENCHREA *(left)*.

REMAINS OF THE OLD HARBOR
AT CENCHREA *(right)*.

AQUEDUCT, CAESAREA.

AND WHEN HE HAD *landed* AT CAESAREA,

AND GONE UP AND *greeted* THE CHURCH,

HE WENT DOWN TO ANTIOCH.

— ACTS 18:22

Caesarea is an important—and beautiful—stop on any tour of Biblical cities. Here, Peter realized that God had opened the door of salvation to the Gentiles (Acts 10:44–48). Paul fled to Caesarea after escaping his enemies shortly after his conversion. He will come here again at the end of his next missionary journey, and again when Felix sends him here for trial.

THE GREAT THEATER.
This structure was in place at the time of Paul.

ROMAN AQUEDUCT AND WATERWHEEL,
ORONTES RIVER, SYRIA.

Paul would have passed this way en route to Antioch.
This area is well known for its waterwheels.

I HAVE BEEN *constantly* ON THE MOVE. I HAVE BEEN IN *danger* FROM RIVERS,

IN DANGER FROM BANDITS, IN DANGER FROM MY OWN COUNTRYMEN,

IN DANGER FROM GENTILES; IN DANGER IN THE CITY, IN DANGER IN

THE COUNTRY, IN DANGER AT SEA; AND IN DANGER FROM

FALSE BROTHERS.... BESIDES EVERYTHING ELSE, I FACE *daily* THE *pressure*

OF MY CONCERN FOR ALL THE CHURCHES. — 2 CORINTHIANS 11:26–28 NIV

Lest we think of Paul as some kind of superman who never grew tired of the road and welcomed constant opposition to his message and threats to his life, his second letter to the Corinthians lets us know he sometimes felt exhausted—tired of walking, tired of sailing, tired of dodging beatings. But in the next chapter, he declares, "I take pleasure in infirmities, in reproaches, in needs, in persecutions, in distresses, for Christ's sake. For when I am weak, then I am strong" (2 Corinthians 12:10). He celebrated and relied on God's grace, which enabled him to carry out the tasks before him.

FISHING BOATS, LAKE EGIRDIR
NEAR PISIDIAN ANTIOCH.

Paul would have passed this lake to or from the city.

AFTER HE HAD SPENT SOME TIME THERE,

HE *departed* AND WENT OVER THE REGION OF GALATIA AND PHRYGIA

IN ORDER, *strengthening* ALL THE DISCIPLES.

— ACTS 18:23

*H*ere Paul began his third missionary journey, returning to the areas he evangelized in Acts 13 and 14. He didn't seem to stay too long in Antioch—or in any single place, for that matter—resting and recuperating. But we know that he relied on the help of others to assist his work. Priscilla and Aquila, Timothy, Silas, and countless others all helped him along the way, and the Philippian church would support him by sending gifts (Philippians 4:10–20). On these journeys, he purposed to strengthen the disciples. And the disciples, in turn, strengthened him.

ANCIENT ROMAN AQUEDUCT, CERTAINLY SEEN BY PAUL.

Pisidian Antioch used to supply water to the city.

WE GIVE *thanks* TO THE GOD AND
FATHER OF OUR LORD JESUS CHRIST,
praying ALWAYS FOR YOU,
SINCE WE HEARD OF YOUR *faith*
IN CHRIST JESUS AND OF
YOUR *love* FOR ALL THE SAINTS.

— PAUL IN HIS LETTER TO THE COLOSSIANS,
A NEARBY CONGREGATION, 1:3–4

FRONTINIUS GATE, ONE OF THE
ENTRY GATES TO THE HIERAPOLIS,
ALONG THE MAIN ROMAN ROAD.

"*Pamukkale*" *means* "*cotton castle,*" and this spot takes its name from the fluffy white cliffs formed by deposits of lime from the surrounding hot springs. When Revelation 3 chastens the church at nearby Laodicea for being "lukewarm, and neither cold nor hot" (v. 16), it might be referring to the contrast of the hot waters here at Hierapolis and the cold waters of Colossae.

But the Christian communities in this area showed distinct signs of zeal and spiritual "heat," so to speak. Paul wrote to the Colossians that "Epaphras, who is one of you . . . has a great zeal for you, and those who are in Laodicea, and those in Hierapolis" (Colossians 4:12–13). And here stands the burial site of the martyr Philip, a testimony to the passion and commitment of the early Christians to the name of Christ, even in the face of death.

AND IT *happened* . . . THAT PAUL,

HAVING PASSED THROUGH THE UPPER REGIONS,

CAME TO EPHESUS.

— ACTS 19:1

*E*phesus was an important place in the Roman world—and in the New Testament. Here is where Paul left Priscilla and Aquila in Acts 18:19, and here Apollos began preaching and teaching (with a little correction from Priscilla and Aquila) in 18:24–28. Timothy ministered here, as Paul certainly did, and John the apostle is said to have lived here. The original site has been uninhabited for centuries, but many of its structures can be seen in ruins, dusty reminders of a rich church history.

(LEFT) THE LIBRARY OF CELCUS,
EPHESUS, TURKEY.

(RIGHT) MOSAIC ON THE FLOOR
OF ONE OF THE UPPER CLASS
ROMAN HOUSES IN EPHESUS
FROM AROUND THE TIME OF PAUL.

ALL WHO *dwelt* IN ASIA

heard THE WORD OF THE LORD,

BOTH JEWS AND GREEKS.

— ACTS 19:10

As Paul ventured among the Gentiles, one of his first tasks was to introduce the Jewish idea of monotheism. Here in Ephesus, he ran into spiritual battles and followers of false gods on a daily basis. The city was home to the temple of Artemis, the earlier name of the widely worshiped Greek goddess Diana, and a conflict arose between Paul and the silversmiths who made shrines of the deity. Their complaints quickly turned into a mob uproar, with chants of "Great is Diana of the Ephesians!" (Acts 19:34).

It certainly wasn't the first time Paul had to contend with the religious landscape of a city—we've already seen his interactions with Corinth. But according to Acts, the Word of the Lord continued to spread. In an earlier section, many people who practiced magic gathered all their magic books and publicly burned them. Luke tells us, "So the word of the Lord grew mightily and prevailed" (19:20).

TEMPLE OF ARTEMIS, EPHESUS.

Storks rest atop one of the remaining pillars
from the temple of Artemis.

THE OLD KAVALA (NEAPOLIS)—
OLD TOWN AND AQUEDUCT.

This is an ancient harbor where Paul would have visited.

AFTER THE *uproar* [AT EPHESUS] HAD CEASED,

PAUL *called* THE DISCIPLES TO HIMSELF, *embraced* THEM,

AND DEPARTED TO GO TO MACEDONIA.

— ACTS 20:1

PILLARS FROM THE ANCIENT HARBOR
OF ALEXANDRIA, TROAS.

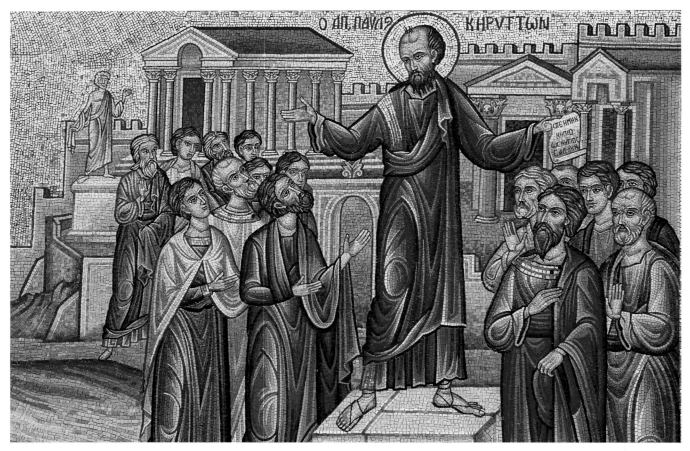

MOSAIC OF PAUL PREACHING
IN OLD CORINTH.

NOW WHEN HE HAD GONE OVER THAT REGION

AND *encouraged* THEM WITH MANY *words,*

HE CAME TO GREECE AND STAYED THREE MONTHS.

— ACTS 20:2–3

This wasn't Paul's first visit to Corinth in Greece, and before arriving he'd kept in close correspondence with the Corinthian Christians via letters. Paul had sharp conflict with this church—they even questioned his apostleship, and it took several letters and visits to iron things out. After they had reconciled and before this three-month stay, he wrote to them 2 Corinthians, full of declarations of God's ability to work mightily in even the humblest human vessel. He might not be the strongest or most powerful man on earth, but by God's grace he carried within him His power for salvation.

STATUE OF ROMAN ARMOR FROM AROUND THE TIME OF PAUL FOUND IN OLD CORINTH.

AND WHEN THE JEWS *plotted* AGAINST HIM

AS HE WAS ABOUT TO SAIL TO SYRIA,

HE DECIDED TO RETURN THROUGH MACEDONIA.

— ACTS 20:3–6

When Dante saw the great apostles in heaven they affected him like *mountains*. There's lots to be said against devotions to saints; but at least they keep on reminding us that we are very small people compared with them. How much smaller before their Master?

— C. S. LEWIS

MOUNT OLYMPUS WITH
VINEYARDS THAT PAUL
WOULD HAVE PASSED.

THE NEXT DAY WE CAME TO MILETUS.

FOR PAUL HAD *decided* TO SAIL PAST EPHESUS,

SO THAT HE WOULD NOT HAVE TO SPEND TIME IN ASIA;

FOR HE WAS *hurrying* TO BE AT JERUSALEM,

IF POSSIBLE, ON THE DAY OF *Pentecost.*

— ACTS 20:15–16

One of the reasons Paul was eager to get to Jerusalem was that he wanted to deliver a gift of money he had been collecting over the course of this third missionary journey. The Jerusalem community may have been hit especially hard by famines in the area, and through his letters to the churches, Paul had gathered a donation. Even as it became apparent that Jerusalem would be a dangerous place for Paul, he was determined to deliver the gift.

THE SACRED WAY AND
IONIC STOA AT
MILETUS, TURKEY.

FROM MILETUS HE SENT TO EPHESUS

AND CALLED FOR THE *elders* OF THE CHURCH.

AND WHEN THEY HAD COME TO HIM, HE SAID TO THEM:

"YOU KNOW, FROM THE FIRST DAY THAT I CAME TO ASIA,

IN WHAT MANNER I ALWAYS LIVED AMONG YOU,

serving THE LORD WITH ALL *humility,*

WITH MANY *tears* AND *trials* WHICH HAPPENED TO ME

BY THE *plotting* OF THE JEWS."

— ACTS 20:17–19

An inscription on the theater at Miletus designates some seats for the Jews or "God-fearing" people. And as Paul's third journey wound to a close, he gathered a group of God-fearers, the Ephesian elders.

Here things took on a slightly different tone—the end of his third missionary journey drew to a close, and his speech recorded in Acts 20:18–35 carries a distinctly torch-passing message. When he closed, he offered a kind of commencement: "So now, brethren, I commend you to God and to the word of His grace, which is able to build you up and give you an inheritance among all those who are sanctified" (v. 32).

When he finished speaking, the elders wept and kissed Paul. Something about the speech made them sure they would never see him again. And while he may well have returned to Asia, the closer he got to Jerusalem, the closer he drew to his final fate.

THE THEATER AT MILETUS.

Paul would have come to and possibly spoken at this theater.

SAINT PAUL'S HARBOR WITH
SAINT PAUL'S CHURCH, LINDOS, RHODES.

NOW IT CAME TO PASS, THAT WHEN WE HAD DEPARTED FROM THEM

AND SET SAIL, RUNNING A *straight* COURSE WE CAME TO COS,

THE FOLLOWING DAY TO RHODES, AND FROM THERE TO PATARA.

AND FINDING A SHIP SAILING OVER TO PHOENICIA,

WE WENT *aboard* AND SET SAIL.

— ACTS 21:1

THE LIGHTHOUSE AT PATARA.

Possibly the oldest in the world, located at the gateway to the old harbor.

Paul's stop in Rhodes gave the harbor its modern title. From there he and his entourage sailed for Patara, another port city, where the Patara lighthouse may have been built sometime around this visit. And when he got to Patara, he changed ships, perhaps hoping to get to Jerusalem faster. That ship would take him on a direct route across the open sea, straight on to Tyre.

WHEN WE HAD SIGHTED CYPRUS,
WE PASSED IT ON THE LEFT, SAILED
TO SYRIA, AND LANDED AT TYRE....
AND *finding* DISCIPLES, WE STAYED
THERE SEVEN DAYS. THEY TOLD PAUL
THROUGH THE *Spirit* NOT TO GO UP
TO JERUSALEM. WHEN WE HAD COME
TO THE END OF THOSE DAYS,
WE DEPARTED AND WENT ON OUR WAY;
AND THEY ALL *accompanied* US,
WITH WIVES AND CHILDREN,
TILL WE WERE OUT OF THE CITY.
AND WE *knelt* DOWN ON THE SHORE
AND PRAYED.

— ACTS 21:3-5

TOMBS OF THE KINGS LOCATED JUST OFF
THE PAPHOS HARBOR IN CYPRUS.

*Paul would have seen these as he passed by on the way to Tyre. Many Christians would
meet in these tombs in times of persecution.*

*I*ncreasingly throughout Acts, the Christian communities coalesce, and we start to get a sense of the Christian family developing—they even call each other "brethren," drawing the scorn of unbelievers. Paul probably didn't know most of these Christians at Tyre, but they spent time with him, prayed with him, and saw him off on his journey nonetheless. The Christians' love for each other, the "bond of perfection" as Paul called it in Colossians 3:14, was powerful enough to strengthen the church even in the face of threat.

BOAT HARBOR AND SEA WALL, PTOLEMAIS.

AND WHEN WE HAD FINISHED OUR *voyage* FROM TYRE,

WE CAME TO PTOLEMAIS, *greeted* THE BRETHREN,

AND STAYED WITH THEM ONE DAY. ON THE NEXT DAY

WE WHO WERE PAUL'S *companions* DEPARTED AND CAME TO CAESAREA.

— ACTS 21:7–8

CAESAREA BEACH, ISRAEL.

*W*hile they stayed at Caesarea, a prophet named Agabus took Paul's belt, bound his hands and feet with it, and said, "So shall the Jews at Jerusalem bind the man who owns this belt" (Acts 21:11). The subtle sense of foreboding here became an explicit prophecy of danger for Paul. But he remained unmoved. Even as his companions pleaded with him to cancel the trip, he said, "What do you mean by weeping and breaking my heart? For I am ready not only to be bound, but also to die at Jerusalem for the name of the Lord Jesus" (21:13).

AND AFTER THOSE DAYS WE PACKED

AND *went up* TO JERUSALEM.

— ACTS 21:15

*This is part of Solomon's Porch.
This is the place of Solomon's Temple,
so Paul would have definitely been in this area.*

It didn't take long, maybe just outside of a week. Shortly after his arrival in Jerusalem, yet another mob uproar erupted around Paul. Jews from Asia saw him and recognized him, and they stirred up a crowd with a barrage of complaints. He taught against the law, they said, and defiled the temple by bringing Gentiles inside (they had seen him with one of the Ephesians and assumed he'd brought him into the temple). They began to beat him, with every intention to kill him, when the commander of the city's Roman garrison interrupted. He couldn't make sense of the Jews' complaints. And so he took Paul into custody.

Paul: The Destiny of a Man

I PRESS TOWARD THE *goal*
FOR THE *prize* OF THE UPWARD *call*
OF GOD IN CHRIST JESUS.

— PHILIPPIANS 3:14

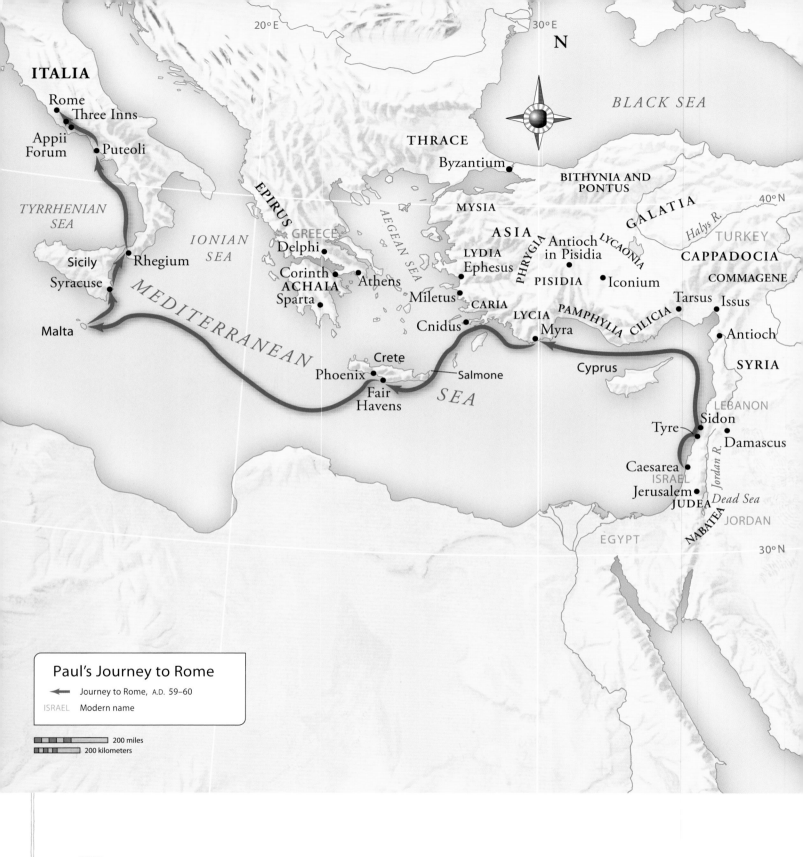

20°E

30°E

N

BLACK SEA

ITALIA

Rome
Three Inns
Appii
Forum
Puteoli

THRACE

Byzantium

**BITHYNIA AND
PONTUS**

*TYRRHENIAN
SEA*

MYSIA

Halys R.

40°N

GALATIA

TURKEY

ASIA

CAPPADOCIA

*IONIAN
SEA*

EPIRUS

GREECE

Delphi

LYDIA
Ephesus

PHRYGIA

Antioch
in Pisidia

LYCAONIA

Sicily

Rhegium

Corinth
ACHAIA
Sparta

Athens

PISIDIA

Iconium

COMMAGENE

Syracuse

Miletus

CARIA

LYCIA

PAMPHYLIA

Tarsus

CILICIA

Issus

Malta

Cnidus

Myra

Cyprus

Antioch

MEDITERRANEAN

Crete

Phoenix

Salmone

SYRIA

Fair
Havens

SEA

LEBANON

Sidon

Tyre

Damascus

Caesarea

ISRAEL

Jordan R.

Jerusalem

JUDEA

Dead Sea

NABATEA

JORDAN

EGYPT

30°N

Paul's Journey to Rome

→ Journey to Rome, A.D. 59–60

ISRAEL   Modern name

▭▭▭▭▭▭ 200 miles
▭▭▭▭▭▭ 200 kilometers

In the Footsteps of Paul

To Rome You Will Go!

IT IS ALMOST UNIVERSALLY ACCEPTED BY BIBLICAL SCHOLARS
THAT PAUL SIGNED HIS OWN DEATH WARRANT WHEN
HE INSISTED ON A TRIAL BEFORE CAESAR.

Three days after Festus became governor, he went from Caesarea to Jerusalem. There the leading priests and the important leaders made *charges* against Paul before Festus. They asked Festus to do them a favor. They wanted him to send Paul back to Jerusalem, because they had a plan to kill him on the way. But Festus answered that Paul would be kept in Caesarea and that he himself was returning there soon. He said, "Some of your leaders should go with me. They can *accuse* the man there in Caesarea, if he has really done something wrong."

Festus stayed in Jerusalem another eight or ten days and then went back to Caesarea. The next day he told the soldiers to bring Paul before him. Festus was seated on the judge's seat when Paul came into the room. The people who had come from Jerusalem stood around him, making serious charges against him, which they could not prove. This is what Paul said to defend himself: "I have done nothing wrong against the law, against the Temple, or against Caesar."

But Festus wanted to please the people. So he asked Paul, "Do you want to go to Jerusalem for me to judge you there on these charges?"

Paul said, "I am standing at Caesar's *judgment* seat now, where I should be judged. I have done nothing wrong to them; you know this is true. If I have done something wrong and the law says I must die, I do not ask to be saved from death. But if these charges are not true, then no one can give me to them. I want Caesar to hear my case!"

Festus talked about this with his advisers. Then he said, "You have asked to see Caesar, so you will go to Caesar!"

— ACTS 25:1-12, NCV

THEY RAISED THEIR *voices* AND SAID,

"AWAY WITH SUCH A FELLOW FROM THE EARTH,

FOR HE IS NOT FIT TO *live!*"

— ACTS 22:22

As Paul stood in Roman chains, attempting to defend himself against the charges of his countrymen, the crowd grew ever more unruly. The commander was unsure of what to do. Paul was a Roman citizen, so he couldn't whip him. He sat him down with the chief priests to try to determine the exact root of the skirmish, but that only ended in more attempted violence against Paul. The Jewish leaders then offered to meet with Paul again—but that was soon revealed to be merely a ploy to murder Paul.

So the commander gathered troops, and sent Paul under guard to Caesarea to be dealt with by the governor.

SUNSET OVER JERUSALEM.

WHEN THEY CAME TO CAESAREA AND HAD *delivered* THE LETTER

TO THE GOVERNOR, THEY ALSO *presented* PAUL TO HIM.

AND WHEN THE GOVERNOR HAD READ IT, HE ASKED WHAT PROVINCE

HE WAS FROM. AND WHEN HE *understood* THAT HE WAS FROM CILICIA,

HE SAID, "I WILL HEAR YOU WHEN YOUR *accusers* HAVE ALSO COME."

AND HE *commanded* HIM TO BE KEPT IN HEROD'S PRAETORIUM.

— ACTS 23:33-35

HIPPODROME, CAESAREA.

With Paul under his jurisdiction, the governor Felix assembled him with two Jewish leaders and asked to hear both sides. Then he delayed making a decision about the case—and delayed, and delayed, in hopes of extracting a bribe from his prisoner. Paul would be imprisoned in Caesarea for two whole years, and Felix never even made a judgment. When his term came to an end, he decided to leave Paul for the next governor.

When Festus succeeded Felix, Paul's enemies were quick to bring up the case again. Festus didn't want to make enemies of these Jews, so he asked Paul if he were willing to go to trial in Jerusalem. But Paul refused, knowing that a trial in the Jewish court wouldn't be fair. He appealed to Caesar, which meant he would be going to Rome.

AND WHEN IT WAS DECIDED THAT WE SHOULD SAIL TO ITALY,

THEY *delivered* PAUL AND SOME OTHER *prisoners* TO ONE

NAMED JULIUS, A CENTURION OF THE AUGUSTAN REGIMENT....

AND THE NEXT DAY WE LANDED AT SIDON.

AND JULIUS TREATED PAUL *kindly* AND GAVE HIM

liberty TO GO TO HIS *friends* AND RECEIVE CARE.

— ACTS 27:1, 3

*H*ere at Sidon Paul's officer let him off the ship to meet with other Christians so that they could give him "care," which presumably means food. At this point, he'd served only a few of what would be several years in prison. Thankfully, God would provide respites like this one, opportunities to receive the loving care of fellow believers.

COMING INTO THE
SIDON HARBOR, LEBANON.

ANDRIKAE PORT, LOCATION OF THE
OLD ENTRY TO MYRA PORT, NEAR
THE RIVER MOUTH LEADING TO MYRA.

*Paul would have sailed from this area. In Paul's day, a thick chain would be
stretched across the river mouth to stop enemies from getting to the city.*

AND WHEN WE HAD *sailed* OVER THE SEA WHICH IS OFF CILICIA

AND PAMPHYLIA, WE CAME TO MYRA, A CITY OF LYCIA.

— ACTS 27:5

At the port of Myra, Paul's centurion found a ship bringing grain from Egypt to Italy. Ships in Paul's day depended on favorable winds. As Paul and the centurion made their way north and west, they relied on winds blowing off the shore from Cilicia and Pamphylia.

ROCK-CUT TOMBS OF MYRA.

Myra is the city from which, later in fourth century, the story of Father Christmas evolved.

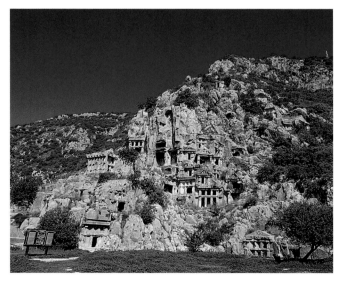

WHEN WE HAD SAILED SLOWLY MANY DAYS,

AND ARRIVED WITH *difficulty* OFF CNIDUS,

THE *wind* NOT PERMITTING US TO PROCEED,

WE SAILED UNDER THE SHELTER OF CRETE OFF SALMONE.

PASSING IT WITH DIFFICULTY, WE CAME TO A PLACE CALLED

FAIR HAVENS, NEAR THE CITY OF LASEA.

— ACTS 27:7–8

SAINT PAUL'S CHURCH, CRETE.

The bay was referred to as "Fair Havens" and is now called Kaloi Limenes. Even today it is a sleepy fishing village. This church is built very close to the Apostle Paul's cave, a small cave where it is believed Paul took shelter during this voyage.

Their ship was struggling. They were traveling outside of the optimal sailing season, and the wind was not allowing them to sail as directly to Italy as they might have hoped. They put in to port at Fair Havens, which, though beautiful, was not the best place to harbor in the winter. So they opted to keep traveling and look for a better port to spend the winter, despite Paul's premonition that "this voyage will end with disaster and much loss" (Acts 27:10).

WHEN THE SOUTH *wind* BLEW SOFTLY, SUPPOSING THAT THEY

HAD OBTAINED THEIR DESIRE, PUTTING OUT TO SEA,

THEY SAILED CLOSE BY CRETE. BUT NOT LONG AFTER,

A *tempestuous* HEAD WIND AROSE, CALLED EUROCLYDON.

— ACTS 27:13–14

The south wind led them to believe it was safe to proceed. But then the wind changed. "Euroclydon" probably refers to a "northeaster"—the kind of wind famous for causing all kinds of trouble. Sure enough, Paul and his shipmates soon found themselves in serious danger.

But Paul received a message from the Lord, and he stood up to address the company: "I urge you to take heart, for there will be no loss of life among you" (Acts 27:22). God had destined him to go before Caesar, and He would spare not only Paul, but everyone on the ship. Their vessel did sink—it ran aground and was battered by the force of the waves. But everyone on board escaped to land, to the island of Malta. To this day, Malta is home to monuments and milestones that mark Paul's visit, one that knocked him off course but wouldn't disrupt his message or his mission.

SAINT PAUL'S GROTTO.

Located where Paul was incarcerated while in Malta.

SAINT PETER AND PAUL'S CATHEDRAL.

The structure is supposedly built on the site of Publius's house.

AND IT HAPPENED THAT THE *father* OF PUBLIUS

LAY SICK OF A *fever* AND *dysentery*.

PAUL WENT IN TO HIM AND PRAYED,

AND HE LAID HIS HANDS ON HIM AND *healed* HIM.

— ACTS 28:8

*L*uke uses the word "unusual" to describe the kindness of the Maltese
(Acts 28:2). And other "unusual" things happened during Paul's stay there. One night a snake latched itself onto his hand, but he remained unharmed, prompting the Maltese to think he was a god. Later, Paul stayed with a leader of the island named Publius, and healed the man's father of a fever by laying hands on him, prompting the other islanders to bring their sick for healing.

What seemed like a digression from the path to Rome still held possibilities for Paul's ministry. He would continue on to his appointment with Caesar, and the scenes of Malta only reinforced that God was with him wherever he went.

AFTER THREE MONTHS WE SAILED IN AN *Alexandrian* SHIP WHOSE FIGUREHEAD WAS THE TWIN BROTHERS, WHICH HAD *wintered* AT THE ISLAND. AND LANDING AT SYRACUSE, WE STAYED THREE DAYS. FROM THERE WE CIRCLED ROUND AND REACHED RHEGIUM. AND AFTER ONE DAY THE SOUTH WIND BLEW; AND THE NEXT DAY WE CAME TO PUTEOLI, WHERE WE *found* BRETHREN, AND WERE *invited* TO STAY WITH THEM SEVEN DAYS. AND SO WE WENT TOWARD ROME.

— ACTS 28:11–13

UNDER THE FLAVIO AMPHITHEATRE IN PUTEOLI, WHERE PAUL WENT AND SPOKE WITH THE BELIEVERS.

Later, Christians were martyred in this amphitheatre for their faith.

*When Paul came to Rhegium it is believed he preached by candlelight—
from a candle which miraculously kept burning. The candle was placed
on a column which today still shows a burn mark.*

*S*yracuse sits on the east of the island of Sicily. Rhegium is on the very toe of the "boot" of Italy; Puteoli is about mid-ankle. Paul would go on foot from Puteoli, growing ever closer to Rome.

VIEW OF SEZZE FROM THE FORUM APPIA.

*Located at the beginning of the Pontine Marshes where Christians
from Rome came to greet Paul.*

AND FROM THERE, WHEN THE *brethren* HEARD ABOUT US, THEY CAME

TO *meet* US AS FAR AS APPII FORUM AND THREE INNS. WHEN PAUL

SAW THEM, HE THANKED GOD AND TOOK *courage.* NOW WHEN WE

CAME TO ROME, THE CENTURION DELIVERED THE *prisoners* TO

THE CAPTAIN OF THE GUARD; BUT PAUL WAS PERMITTED TO *dwell*

BY HIMSELF WITH THE SOLDIER WHO GUARDED HIM. — ACTS 28:15–16

The men who guarded Paul seemed to think well of him and trust him. Back in Caesarea, the governor Festus and his friends even said, "This man is doing nothing deserving of death or chains" (Acts 26:31). The state officials with whom Paul interacted all seemed to hope this religious conflict within Judaism could be worked out, and surely Paul would not have to die.

But there was a problem, of course. Paul had appealed to Caesar and was determined to be heard by him. To make matters worse, the emperor Nero was slowly descending into madness. He couldn't be counted on to deal justly and reasonably with the early Christians.

THE APPIAN WAY IN THE AREA WHERE THE THREE TAVERNS WERE LOCATED.

This is the land route by which Paul approached Rome.

AND *it came to pass* AFTER THREE DAYS

THAT PAUL CALLED THE *leaders*

OF THE JEWS TOGETHER.

— ACTS 28:17

*P*aul's last recorded speech in Acts is his discourse with the Roman Jews. Maybe he was hoping to gain their favor before he went before Caesar, or maybe he wanted to make amends. Certainly, though, he wanted to preach the gospel. More than anything, he wanted to see his fellow Jews embrace God's salvation through Christ.

The results were the same as most any other time he preached: some were convinced, others argued. But Paul stayed true to his mission, speaking the word of God, whatever the outcome.

THE STADIUM OF DOMITIAN
AT PALATINO HILL.

Paul would have seen this area.

QVESTA É LA COLONNA DOVE STANDO
LEGATI I SS·APOSTOLI PIETRO E PAOLO
CONVERTIRNO I SS·MARTIRI PROCESSO
E MARTINIANO CVSTODI DELLE CARCERI ET
ALTRI XLVI·ALLA FEDE DI CRISTO QVALI
BATTEZZORNO COLL·ACQVA DI QVESTO
FONTE SCATVRITA MIRACOLOSAMENTE

THEN PAUL *dwelt* TWO YEARS IN HIS OWN RENTED HOUSE,

AND RECEIVED ALL WHO CAME TO HIM,

preaching THE KINGDOM OF GOD

AND *teaching* THE THINGS WHICH CONCERN

THE LORD JESUS CHRIST WITH ALL CONFIDENCE,

NO ONE FORBIDDING HIM.

— ACTS 28:30 – 31

Acts ends rather abruptly, with Paul under house arrest for two years, and the details of his life after those two years are a little sketchy. Did his case go before Caesar as planned, or did it reach its statute of limitations, enabling Paul to go free? If he went free, did he continue his missionary journeys, and if so, where?

We might not know exactly what the rest of Paul's life looked like, but according to tradition, he and Peter were arrested and imprisoned here in Rome at Mamertine Prison under Nero's rabid persecution of Christians. Paul was then beheaded and died a martyr's death.

We're not sure why Luke neglected to tell us how Paul died. But maybe his ending is a perfectly appropriate picture of Paul's fate: it shows him preaching the gospel of Christ in the face of all persecution, until the very, very last.

THE MAMERTINE PRISON WHERE BOTH
PETER AND PAUL WERE IMPRISONED.

From this well they would have drunk water, and the pillar by the altar was where they were chained. Water from this well was used to baptize the prisoners and guards.

SAINT PAUL'S AT THREE FOUNTAINS,
OUTSIDE OF ROME.

*It is believed Paul was beheaded here. According to tradition, when he was beheaded,
his head bounced three times and three fountains sprung up from the earth.*

FOR I AM ALREADY BEING POURED OUT AS A DRINK OFFERING,

AND THE TIME OF MY DEPARTURE IS AT HAND.

I HAVE FOUGHT THE *good fight*, I HAVE *finished the race*,

I HAVE *kept the faith.*

— PAUL TO TIMOTHY IN 2 TIMOTHY 4:6–7

The definitive biography of [Paul] is yet to be written and may never be written. But were the apostle to have written an autobiography, without doubt he would have stressed the cruciform and christocentric pattern of his life. He stood in the shadow of the Galilean and not infrequently reflected the character of the One he served. No higher compliment can be paid to a Christian than to say he lived out of and strove to emulate the story of Christ.

— BEN WITHERINGTON III

THE PILLAR ON WHICH PAUL WAS BEHEADED.

Located at the Church of Saint Paul at the Three Fountains.

[ACKNOWLEDGMENTS]

Page 19, Dietrich Bonhoeffer, The Cost of Discipleship (New York: Simon and Schuster, 1995), 203.

Page 23, Eugene H. Peterson, Traveling Light, God's Message for Each Day (Nashville: J. Countryman, 2004), 18.

Page 27, Max Lucado, The Applause of Heaven (Dallas: Word Publishing, 1990), 39–41.

Page 29, William Barclay, The Acts of the Apostles, rev. ed., The New Daily Study Bible, rev. ed. (Louisville, KY: Westminster John Knox Press, 2003), 83.

Page 31, Philip Yancey, What's So Amazing About Grace? (Grand Rapids, Mich.: Zondervan, 1997), 66.

Page 35, F. F. Bruce, In the Steps of the Apostle Paul (Grand Rapids, Mich.: Kregel, 1995), 14.

Page 37, Richard Exley, Blue Collar Christianity (Tulsa, Okla.: Honor Books, 1989), 48.

Page 41, Rick Warren, The Purpose Driven Life (Grand Rapids, Mich.: Zondervan, 2002), 222.

Page 47, Justo L. Gonzalez, The Story of Christianity (San Francisco: HarperSanFrancisco, 1984), 31.

Page 59, Henri Nouwen, Spiritual Direction: Wisdom for the Long Walk of Faith (San Francisco: HarperSanFrancisco, 2006), 142.

Page 75, Thomas Merton, No Man Is an Island (San Diego: Harcourt Brace & Company, 1983), 131.

Page 81, Billy Graham, Unto the Hills (Waco, TX: Word Books, 1986), 192.

Page 89, Beth Moore, To Live Is Christ (Nashville: Broadman & Holman, 2001), 112.

Page 95, C. H. Spurgeon, The Best of C. H. Spurgeon (Grand Rapids, Mich.: Baker Books, 1977), 108–109.

Page 101, John Piper, Pierced by the Word (Sisters, Ore.: Multnomah, 2003), 122.

Page 107, N. T. Wright, Simply Christian (San Francisco: HarperSanFrancisco, 2006), 133–134.

Page 133, C. S. Lewis, The Business of Heaven, The Inspirational Writings of C. S. Lewis (New York: Inspirational Press, 1994), 399.

Page 171, Ben Witherington III, The Paul Quest (Downers Grove, Ill: InterVarsity Press, 1998), 303.

ALSO FROM KEN DUNCAN

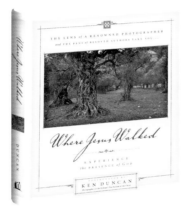 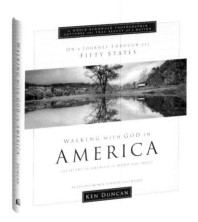

Where Jesus Walked

VISIT THE PLACES WHERE JESUS LIVED AND DIED AND ROSE AGAIN, THROUGH THE LENS OF A WORLD RENOWNED PHOTOGRAPHER.

Walking with God in America

DISCOVER FOR YOURSELF THAT AMERICA'S BEAUTY IS A REFLECTION OF GOD'S BLESSING.